HAIL to Spring!

PICTURE WINDOW BOOKS
a capstone imprint

by

illustrated by
Laura Watson

Springtime lightning flashes, soars.

Springtime thunder rumbles, roars.

Storms bring hail that falls like rain ...

4

rapping, tapping on the pane.

Balls of hail fall on the trees ...

dashing, crashing through the leaves.

Plinking, clinking on the car ...

13

hail is falling near and far.

Shimmering, glimmering in the street ...

hail is dancing at our feet.

Sunshine melts the hail away.
We all run outside to play!

Time to laugh. Time to sing.
Time to say, "Hail to spring!"

- Hail is a solid form of precipitation. Precipitation is rain, snow, sleet, or hail that falls to the ground from clouds.

- Hail forms in cumulonimbus clouds. Cumulonimbus clouds produce thunderstorms.

- Hail freezes while it is in a cloud. Once the ball of ice falls to the ground, it is called a hailstone. Hailstones can be as small as a pea or as large as a tennis ball.

- Hailstorms can be dangerous. During a storm, stay indoors.

Cumulonimbus Cloud

anvil top

dark base

All the Titles in This Set:

Hail to Spring!

Raindrops Fall All Around

Sunshine Brightens Springtime

A Windy Day in Spring

Internet Sites

FactHound offers a safe, fun way to find Internet sites related to this book. All of the sites on FactHound have been researched by our staff.

Here's all you do:

Visit www.facthound.com

Type in this code: 9781479560295

Super-cool stuff! Check out projects, games and lots more at www.capstonekids.com

For Charlotte and Christopher.

Thanks to our adviser for his expertise, research, and advice:
Terry Flaherty, PhD, Professor of English
Minnesota State University, Mankato

Editors: Shelly Lyons and Elizabeth R. Johnson
Designer: Lori Bye
Art Director: Nathan Gassman
Production Specialist: Tori Abraham

The illustrations in this book were created with acrylics and digital collage.

Picture Window Books are published by Capstone,
1710 Roe Crest Drive, North Mankato, Minnesota 56003
www.capstonepub.com

Library of Congress Cataloging-in-Publication Data
Ghigna, Charles, author.
Hail to spring! / by Charles Ghigna ; illustrated by Laura Watson.
pages cm. — (Nonfiction picture books. Springtime weather wonders)
  Summary: "Introduces hail through fun, poetic text and colorful illustrations"—Provided by publisher.
  Audience: Ages 5-7.
  Audience: K to grade 3.
ISBN 978-1-4795-6029-5 (library binding : alk. paper)
ISBN 978-1-4795-6033-2 (big book)
ISBN 978-1-4795-6037-0 (ebook pdf)
ISBN 978-1-4795-6041-7 (board book)
1. Spring—Juvenile literature. 2. Hail—Juvenile literature. 3. Weather—Juvenile literature.
I. Watson, Laura, 1968- illustrator. II. Title.

Design Elements
Shutterstock. R2D2

QB637.5.G483 2015
508.2—dc23   2014029004

Printed in Canada.
092014   008478FRS15